UGLY CHRISTMAS SWEATER PARTY

CHRISTMAS CRAFTS, RECIPES, ACTIVITIES

BRANDY & MATT SHAY

LARK
New York

LARK
New York

An Imprint of Sterling Publishing
1166 Avenue of the Americas
New York, NY 10036

ISBN 978-1-4547-0989-3

Distributed in Canada by Sterling Publishing Co., Inc.
c/o Canadian Manda Group, 664 Annette Street
Toronto, Ontario, Canada M6S 2C8
Distributed in the United Kingdom by GMC Distribution Services
Castle Place, 166 High Street, Lewes, East Sussex, England BN7 1XU
Distributed in Australia by Capricorn Link (Australia) Pty. Ltd.
P.O. Box 704, Windsor, NSW 2756, Australia

For information about custom editions, special sales, and premium and corporate purchases,
please contact Sterling Special Sales at 800-805-5489 or specialsales@sterlingpublishing.com.

Manufactured in China

2 4 6 8 10 9 7 5 3 1

larkcrafts.com

Ugly Christmas Sweater Party

We wanted to thank our ugly-sweater-wearing family and friends for helping us research the projects within this book. Every year we have an ugly sweater Christmas party to raise money to help a family in need over the holiday season.

Throughout the years, I am happy to say we have raised thousands of dollars to make the season a little brighter for some that could use a helping hand. We are proud to be a part of this ugly-sweater-wearing crew! We dedicate this book to each and every one of you who have participated over the years!

Thank You!
Brandy and Matt

UGLY CONTENTS

'TWAS THE NIGHT BEFORE THE UGLY SWEATER SOIREE

AND ALL THROUGH YOUR PLACE,

YOUR PERFECT PARTY CLOTHES WERE PUT AWAY WITHOUT EVEN A TRACE.

YOUR GUESTS WILL DRINK CRANBERRY COCKTAILS AND CRAFT,

WHILE WEARING SWEATERS THAT ARE ZANY AND DAFT.

YOU WILL DISPLAY MARSHMALLOWS AND CANDY CANES TO LOOK NICE AND PRETTY,

AND YOUR FRIENDS MAY EVEN DECIDE TO BELT OUT A DITTY.

AS THEY MODEL THEIR HEINOUS PARTY ATTIRE,

THEY'LL HOPE TO WIN PRIZES FOR THE MOST HOPELESSLY DIRE.

YES, FOR THIS SHINDIG PLEASE LEAVE YOUR CHIC STYLE AT HOME,

AND COME DRESSED IN THE UGLIEST CHRISTMAS SWEATER YOU OWN.

FOR THE WHOLE POINT IS CLEARLY TO EAT, DRINK, AND BE MERRY,

SO DON'T FRET, YOU'LL WITHOUT DOUBT LOOK LIKE A GIANT STRAWBERRY.

SO COME ONE, COME ALL, TO THE UGLY SWEATER SOIREE!

KICK BACK, RELAX, AND GET CARRIED AWAY!

Admit it, you'd love to host an ugly sweater party this holiday season. But aside from donning your craziest Christmas clothes, you really have no idea how to plan one . . . until now. Set the date, friends, because in this field guide we've done all the work for you. Inside you will find everything you need for the ugliest party you could throw, and we mean that in the nicest way possible. From irresistibly festive invites to enticing eats and drinks, plus party games (candy cane pickup, anyone?), prizes, and cute crafts (who doesn't need an ugly ornament drinking glass in their life?), we've got you covered. So start thinking about who's on your nice list, and then read on for the tips and tricks you'll need. 'Tis the season!

Food & Drink

Ugly Sweater Cake

This knitted sweater cake would make even Grandma proud! Don't be afraid, it's easier than it looks!

INGREDIENTS

Cake recipe

Large gift box

Parchment paper

Tissue paper

Frosting

Food coloring

Cookie cutters

Icing bag and small round tip, or airtight bag with cut-off corner

Candies for embellishments

INSTRUCTIONS

1. Bake cake according to your recipe and let cool.

2. Cut cake to fit inside the gift box. Line the gift box with parchment paper strips that can easily be removed. Place tissue paper inside the gift box. After the gift box is prepared, place the cake inside.

3. Color frosting with desired sweater colors. Cover cake with a layer of the main frosting color.

4. Using cookie cutters, make small impressions wherever you want your sweater designs.

5. In a small back-and-forth motion, pipe small lines across the cake to resemble the rows of a knitted sweater. Try to keep the rows as straight as possible, going around the impressions. Refrigerate for 1 hour to set the icing.

6. Add different colors of frosting over the impressions in the same back-and-forth motion. Refrigerate again, and then embellish with candy and other icing colors.

7. Before serving, remove parchment paper and touch up borders with extra icing. Accept compliments.

FOOD & DRINK

Ugly Cake Pops

These little chocolate-covered wonders are the perfect bite. They're great for holiday dieters who say, "Oh, I can't have a whole slice. I'll just have one of these little pops." Little do they know, they'll end up eating thirty!

INGREDIENTS

1 box of your favorite cake mix and ingredients to make it

1 container pre-made frosting in a coordinating flavor

Miniature cookie scoop or tablespoon

Cookie sheet

Parchment paper

2 packages of your favorite color of melting chocolate

Glass microwave-safe bowl

Cooking oil

Lollipop sticks

Tweezers

Decorative sprinkles

Floral styrofoam to hold finished pops

14

INSTRUCTIONS

1. Bake your cake according to the package instructions and let cool.

2. Crumble the cake into a large mixing bowl using your hands. Add about half the can of frosting and stir with a spoon until a large ball forms and the sides of the bowl are clean. Add more frosting as needed, but keep in mind that it's easier to add frosting than to bake another cake to crumble.

3. Using a miniature cookie scoop or tablespoon, measure out a small amount of cake into your hand, and roll it into a small ball. Place on a cookie sheet covered in parchment paper. Continue making cake balls with the rest of the cake mixture, then place the cookie sheet in the freezer for 10 minutes.

4. While you're waiting, microwave chocolate in a glass bowl on half power. Melt in 45-second increments, stirring in between, until chocolate coats a spoon and is the texture of cake batter. If it is too thick, add a little hot cooking oil 1 tablespoon at a time. Be careful not to overheat the chocolate or it will scorch and clump up!

5. Transfer cake balls into the fridge and let the chocolate cool to almost room temperature. Place sprinkles in separate bowls and get the lollipop sticks ready to go.

6. Take four or five cake balls out of the fridge. Dip a lollipop stick in chocolate then insert it about ¾ inch into a cake ball. When the stick is secure, dip the cake ball all the way into the chocolate in one plunging motion. Remove cake ball from the chocolate and tap the stick on your opposite hand to let excess chocolate drip back into the chocolate bowl. Put the stick into floral foam to let the chocolate harden. Repeat for remaining cake balls. If your cake pops crack, try thinning out the chocolate or taking cake balls out of the fridge sooner. Don't double-dip as it will cause cracking.

7. To add sprinkles, dip a toothpick into melted chocolate and apply to the cake ball as glue, then add sprinkles with tweezers. Stick completed cake balls into floral foam to finish drying.

8. If desired, drizzle a coordinating color of melted chocolate over your cake balls using a spoon and a quick hand!

Red Velvet Cupcakes

Nothing is more festive than red velvet cake for the holidays! Red velvet comes from the South. It's actually a chocolate cake with a whole lot of red food coloring or even beet juice added for color. You can purchase a boxed mix, but if you choose to make them from scratch, gel food coloring is recommended as it's more potent. You'll need a whole 3-ounce container.

INGREDIENTS

Your favorite red velvet cake recipe, or a boxed mix and ingredients to make it

Cupcake liners

Cupcake pan

Ice cream scoop

Your favorite cream cheese frosting recipe

Piping bag with large star tip (3M or 1M)

Decorative sprinkles

INSTRUCTIONS

1. Mix cake ingredients. Line cupcake pan with cupcake liners and fill with cake batter. Fill liners using an ice cream scoop to make sure all the cupcakes will be uniform. If you have empty spots in your pan, fill with water to ensure even baking. Bake according to your recipe and let cool.

2. Prepare the frosting and fill the piping bag. Pipe icing onto cupcakes. Begin in the middle and move in a counterclockwise circle, ending up in the middle again for the perfect swirl.

3. To pipe two different colors in a swirl, prepare two small piping bags with different colors of frosting; no tips are needed. Place both bags inside a larger bag fitted with a star tip. Swirl in the same manner.

4. Top cupcakes with sprinkles.

Strawberry Santa Hats

Top the night off with this guilty pleasure. These little Santa hats will have all your guests feeling festive and jolly.

INGREDIENTS

1 package store-bought brownie bites

1 can whipped cream

1 package fresh strawberries

INSTRUCTIONS

1. Spray a brownie bite with whipped cream.

2. Use a knife to cut off the top of a strawberry.

3. Stick the fat end of the strawberry onto the brownie.

4. Use whipped cream to make the ball on Santa's cap.

Ugly Rice Cereal Tree

Decorate this yummy crispy treat, and you won't have to worry about taking it down when the party is over. The ugly sweater elves will devour these after trying one little taste, making this tree cleanup super simple!

INGREDIENTS

1 pan of rice cereal treats made with green food coloring

1 small package of your favorite candy to decorate the tree

Festive ornament

INSTRUCTIONS

1. Make your favorite rice cereal treat recipe with added green food coloring.

2. Cut the treats into squares.

3. Arrange them on a platter in a pyramid shape with more squares at the bottom, gradually getting smaller toward the top.

4. Use candies to decorate the tree.

5. Put the ornament on top.

Ugly Sweater Cookies

What's better than sugar cookies—especially cute ones that double as fashion?

INGREDIENTS

Sugar cookie recipe

Sweater cookie cutter

Royal icing

Cookie icing

Cookie sheet lined with parchment paper

Piping bag

Decorative sprinkles

INSTRUCTIONS

1. Make your favorite sugar cookie dough. Place in a bowl and cover with plastic wrap. Chill for at least 2 hours.

2. Roll out to ¼ inch thick and cut out shapes using a sweater cookie cutter.

3. Bake according to your recipe on a cookie sheet lined with parchment paper, and let cool.

4. Using royal icing and a small tip, pipe a thin border around cookies then let dry until stiff.

5. Use cookie icing to fill in cookies. Be careful not to use too much or it will leak over the borders. After squeezing a small amount, use the tip to spread icing close to the border and let it spread.

6. Let dry about 20 minutes, then add sprinkles. Get creative! You're not just a baker, you're a fashion designer!

Candy Cane Pizza

You'll need oven mitts instead of stockings for this tasty, pepperoni-striped delight.

INGREDIENTS

½ cup flour

1 ball pre-made pizza dough

Nonstick cooking spray

½ cup pizza sauce

½ cup mozzarella cheese

1 package sliced pepperoni

INSTRUCTIONS

1. Sprinkle flour on your counter so the pizza dough will not stick.

2. Roll pizza dough out until it is ¼ inch thick. If you like your pizza crust thinner, roll it out more.

3. Put rolled-out pizza dough on a baking sheet sprayed with nonstick cooking spray. Use a knife to lightly draw the shape of a candy cane. Re-draw it if necessary until you are happy with it. Use a pizza cutter to cut out the shape.

4. Preheat oven to 400 degrees.

5. Use a spoon to spread pizza sauce over the candy-cane-shaped dough.

6. Sprinkle a generous amount of cheese on the pizza.

7. Place sliced pepperoni on the candy cane in rows to create the candy cane stripes.

8. Bake in preheated oven for 12–14 minutes or until the cheese is melted and the edges of the pizza are golden brown.

FOOD & DRINK

Christmas Tree Pizza

The toppings were hung by the oven with care, in hopes the hungry sweater-wearers soon would be there.

INGREDIENTS

½ cup flour

1 ball pre-made pizza dough

Nonstick cooking spray

½ cup pizza sauce

½ cup shredded mozzarella

½ cup sliced green olives

½ cup diced red pepper

1 yellow pepper

INSTRUCTIONS

1. Sprinkle flour on your counter so the pizza dough will not stick.

2. Roll pizza dough out until it is ¼ inch thick. If you like your pizza crust thinner, roll it out more.

3. Put rolled-out pizza dough on a baking sheet sprayed with nonstick cooking spray. Use a knife to lightly draw the shape of a Christmas tree. Re-draw it if necessary until you are happy with it.

4. Use a pizza cutter to cut out the shape.

5. Preheat oven to 400 degrees.

6. Use a spoon to spread pizza sauce over the tree-shaped dough.

7. Sprinkle a generous amount of cheese on the pizza.

8. Place green olives in straight lines across the tree as a garland.

9. Add diced red peppers onto the tree as red Christmas lights.

10. Cut the yellow pepper in the shape of a star and place it on top.

11. Bake in preheated oven for 12–15 minutes or until the cheese is melted and the edges of the pizza are golden brown.

Pigs in an Ugly Sweater Wreath

Wrap up miniature hot dogs in an "ugly sweater" wreath to make this tasty treat. These are sure to be a hit with all who try!

INGREDIENTS

½ cup flour

2 cans pre-made crescent dough

2 packages hotdogs

Nonstick cooking spray

Christmas flower or bow

INSTRUCTIONS

1. Preheat oven to 375 degrees.

2. Sprinkle flour over your counter.

3. Pop open the crescent dough.

4. Starting at the large end of a dough triangle, roll a hotdog inside. Repeat for all crescents.

5. Place rolled hotdogs on a cookie sheet sprayed with nonstick cooking spray with the ends of each triangle underneath.

6. Bake 12–14 minutes or until golden brown.

7. Arrange on a platter in a circle. Decorate with a Christmas flower or bow.

Frosty the Cheese Ball

Frosty the cheese ball will give your guests a happy soul, with a carrot nose, crackers, and some cloves.

INGREDIENTS

3 cheese balls

Cloves

1 green onion

1 carrot

1 package of your favorite crackers

Small top hat

INSTRUCTIONS

1. Combine then mold the cheese balls into one large, medium, and small cheese ball.

2. Arrange cheese balls on a platter from largest to smallest.

3. Use the cloves as the buttons, eyes, and mouth.

4. Cut off the end of the carrot, and shave it into a smaller carrot. Add to the small cheese ball for a nose.

5. Add the green end of the scallion as a scarf.

6. Lay crackers around the snowman.

7. Put a small top hat on the snowman.

Ugly Sweater Grinch Punch

With a punch this tasty, you won't want to stop Christmas from coming . . . in fact, you'll be upset it's only once a year.

INGREDIENTS

1 cup orange juice

1 cup blue caraçao

1 (12-oz) light beer

2 liters lemon-lime soda

3 limes, juiced

½ cup fresh cranberries

INSTRUCTIONS

1. Pour all ingredients into a large punch bowl.
2. Garnish with fresh cranberries.

UGLY SWEATER
GRINCH PUNCH

Elf Punch in the Gut

Whether you've been naughty or nice, these fruity flavors will leave you in the mood for another punch.

INGREDIENTS

1 cup orange juice

1 cup lemonade

1 bottle champagne

1 cup cranberry juice

1 cup cranberry-flavored vodka

2 liters ginger ale

1 lemon, thinly sliced

4 sprigs rosemary

½ cup fresh cranberries

INSTRUCTIONS

1. Pour first six ingredients into a large punch bowl.
2. Garnish with lemon slices, rosemary sprigs, and cranberries.

Peppermint Eggnog Twister
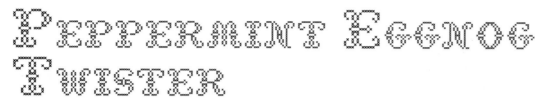

Cuddle up with this warm minty cup of holiday cheer. All of your ugly-sweater guests will be fighting over the rim for this white chocolate wonder.

INGREDIENTS

½ cup white chocolate chips, melted

1 candy cane, smashed

1 shot peppermint schnapps

1 shot Southern Comfort®

Eggnog

1 whole candy cane

DIRECTIONS

1. Melt white chocolate chips on a plate in the microwave.
2. Tip a mug upside down into the white chocolate to coat it.
3. Sprinkle the rim with candy cane dust.
4. Pour liquor into the mug.
5. Fill the rest of the mug with your favorite eggnog.
6. Garnish with a candy cane.

Make it a Peppermint Eggnog Shooter

INGREDIENTS

½ oz peppermint schnaps

½ oz Southern Comfort®

Eggnog

Whipped cream

1 candy cane, smashed

DIRECTIONS

1. In a large shot glass combine the schnapps and Southern Comfort®.

2. Top with eggnog.

3. Spray whipped cream on top.

4. Sprinkle with candy cane dust.

33

Kris-Cran Kringle Margarita

The big guy has headed south, of the border that is, to bring you this festive treat. Nothing will get you in the holiday spirit like tequila and cranberries.

INGREDIENTS

Rock salt

Ice cubes

1½ oz tequila

1 oz orange liquor

½ cup lemon-lime soda

2 oz cranberry juice

½ lime, juiced

6 fresh cranberries

1 slice lime

INSTRUCTIONS

1. Wet top of a margarita glass with water and sprinkle with rock salt.

2. Put ice in a shaker.

3. Pour tequila and orange liquor over ice in the shaker and shake until cold.

4. Pour mixture into margarita glass until one-fourth full.

5. Top with lemon-lime soda and cranberry juice.

6. Add cranberries in the glass and a lime slice on the rim.

Jingle Bells Sangria

Hear them ring, ring-a-ding-ding! As you sip this scrumptious sangria, you'll ring in ugly holiday cheer.

INGREDIENTS

1 bottle red wine

1 cup vodka

1 cup pomegranate juice

1 cup orange juice

½ cup pomegranate arils

½ cup fresh cranberries

1 orange, thinly sliced

1 cinnamon stick

2 liters ginger ale

INSTRUCTIONS

1. Pour wine, vodka, and juices into a large pitcher.

2. Add pomegranate arils, cranberries, orange slices, and cinnamon stick.

3. To serve, pour into large wine glass until three-fourths full and top with ginger ale.

JINGLE
BELLS
SANGRIA

Pumpkin Ugly-Nogg Martini

Your ugly-sweater friends will ask for this martini shaken, not stirred. Then they'll be back to take it any way they can get it, with sugar and spice and everything nice.

INGREDIENTS

1 tsp cinnamon

1 TB sugar

1½ oz spiced rum

1 oz vanilla vodka

3½ oz pumpkin-flavored eggnog

Ice cubes

Cinnamon stick

INSTRUCTIONS

1. Wet rim of a martini glass with water.

2. Mix cinnamon and sugar on a plate, and dip the rim of the glass into the cinnamon and sugar.

3. Put remaining ingredients over ice in a shaker and shake until cold.

4. Pour drink mixture in the rimmed martini glass.

5. Sprinkle extra cinnamon and sugar in the drink and garnish with a cinnamon stick.

The Blue Christmas

Even Elvis wouldn't be blue after tasting this frosty delight. Go ahead and add some blue to your Christmas. You'll be doin' all right.

INGREDIENTS

1 TB sugar

Ice cubes

2 oz vodka

1 oz blue liqueur

1 oz lime juice

1 oz orange liquor

Decorative snowflake or candy snowflake charms

INSTRUCTIONS

1. Wet rim of a martini glass with water.

2. Put sugar on a plate, and dip the rim of the glass in the sugar to coat it.

3. Combine ice and remaining ingredients in shaker and shake until cold.

4. Pour drink mixture into sugar-rimmed glass.

5. Garnish with a decorative snowflake or candy snowflake charms.

Santa's Fire Cider

After a long night on the job, even Saint Nick needs a pick-me-up. Fire one up, for a long ugly winter's night.

INGREDIENTS

Ice cubes

1½ oz cinnamon whiskey

½ bottle apple cider beer

Ginger ale

Apple slice

Cinnamon stick

Cinnamon, to garnish

INSTRUCTIONS

1. Fill a rocker glass with ice.

2. Pour in the cinnamon whiskey and hard cider.

3. Top with ginger ale.

4. Sprinkle cinnamon on apple slice and place on the side of the glass. Add a cinnamon stick.

Festive Champagne Punch

This bright flute of fun will keep the elves in the workshop, whistling and bubbling while they work.

INGREDIENTS

Sugar: green and red

Pineapple juice

Cranberry juice

Champagne

INSTRUCTIONS

1. Wet rims of champagne flutes with water.

2. Spread sugars onto a plate, and dip each rim into red or green sugar.

3. Fill one-third of each champagne flute with cranberry juice.

4. Fill another third of each flute with pineapple juice.

5. Top off each flute with champagne.

Peppermint Popper

You won't go silent into the night after this minty little popper. It will have you popping around in your ugliest of garb. All won't be calm, but it sure will be bright.

INGREDIENTS

1 oz mint liquor

1 oz Irish cream

Whipped cream

Rosemary sprig

INSTRUCTIONS

1. Fill a large shot glass with mint liquor and Irish cream.

2. Top with whipped cream.

3. Garnish with a rosemary sprig.

Russian to Get Ugly

You'll need a furry hat to go with your sweater after this boastful beverage.

INGREDIENTS

Ice cubes

2 oz vanilla vodka

1 oz coffee liquor

Eggnog

Cinnamon, to garnish

INSTRUCTIONS

1. Fill a rocker glass with ice.

2. Pour in the vanilla vodka and coffee liquor.

3. Top with eggnog.

4. Sprinkle with cinnamon to garnish.

45

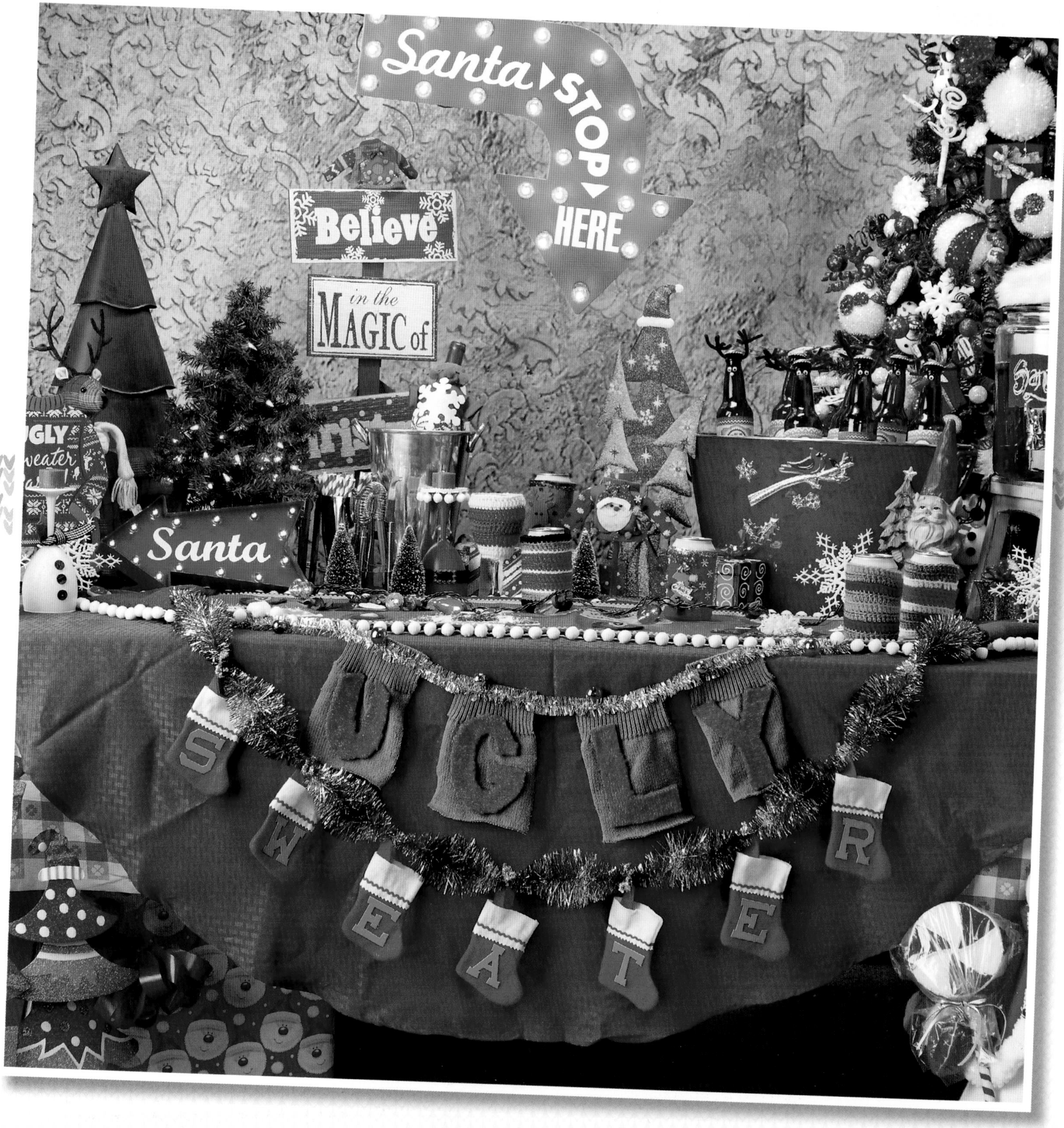
Santa STOP HERE
Believe
in the MAGIC of
Santa
UGLY
SWEATER

Hideous Projects

Ugly Sweater Bunting & Garland

This bunting garland is a must-have for your holiday hoorah! Display these together across an ugly table spread, on your front door to welcome guests, or on the wall for an additional spot to take photos.

SUPPLIES

Doodlebug Design glitter cardstock

Hot glue gun

Marker

Metallic piper cleaners

Mini felt stockings

Scissors

Silhouette Cameo craft cutter

Sweaters: 1 red and 1 green

Tinsel garlands: 1 silver and 1 multicolored

INSTRUCTIONS

1. Cut up a green sweater into 5" x 6" squares. Draw the word "Ugly" in thick letters onto the red sweater, and cut out.

2. Hot-glue the letters onto the green squares. Hot-glue silver tinsel garland across the tops of the "Ugly" green banner squares.

3. Bend pipe cleaners into one letter at a time and hot-glue them in place.

4. Using a craft cutter, cut out the word "Sweater" from green glitter cardstock, and hot-glue each letter to a mini stocking.

5. Tie the mini stockings to the multicolored tinsel garland using pipe cleaners.

HIDEOUS PROJECTS

"Felt Ugly" Table Runner

This little gem will surely ugly up your festive table design with ugly sweaters, glitter, and pompoms. Just wait until your guests take a look at this!

SUPPLIES

Assorted small buttons

Fabric Cutter, or circle template

Embroidery floss: red, white, and green

Fabric glue and/or glue gun

Felt: 72" wide, ⅓ yd red, ⅓ yd white, and ⅓ yd green

Green tinsel

Iron-on patches

Large button

Lime-green mini pompom trim: 2½ yds

Mini Christmas trims

Mini jingle bells

Needle and strong thread

Ribbons

Rickrack

Santa hat

Sewing machine

Sparkly felt: 72" wide, ½ yd green, ½ yd red and ⅓ yd lime green

White pompom trim: 3½ yds

INSTRUCTIONS

1. Cut one 15½" x 58" piece of the sparkly green felt and one 13½" x 58" piece of sparkly red felt. Cut two sweater shapes each from the lime-green, green, and white felt. Cut out an assortment of circles in the following sizes and colors: two red, two dark green, and two lime-green 3-inch circles; two red, two white, one lime-green, and one dark green 2-inch circles; and two white, two dark green, one red, and one lime-green 1-inch circles.

2. Measure 7 inches down from each end of the red sparkly fabric; this allows enough space for the green fabric to fold over the top. Place a pin on each of these areas so you know not to sew there. Determine the placement you'd like for the sweaters and dots, pin them in place, and then sew them down. Using embroidery floss, sew an "X" in each of the 1-inch circles in contrasting colors.

3. Use your imagination and trims to create and decorate the tackiest sweaters you can! I hand-sewed some of the trims down and also used a glue gun and fabric glue.

4. To sew the table runner together, put the red sparkly felt and the green sparkly felt right sides together along the long edges. Sew using a ¼-inch seam allowance on both sides, and then turn right side out to create a long tube. Center the red piece with the green piece (you'll have a long green seam along the red center) and press. At each end, fold the tube wrong sides together and stitch at the top with a ¼-inch seam allowance. When both ends are sewn, turn them each inside out to reveal a triangle end on each side of the table runner. Sew a decorative button on each end.

5. Using a glue gun, glue the pompom trim around the bottom of the table runner, keeping the edges straight. Glue the green trim next, making sure it's straight along the seams. Sew two large buttons to each end, and you're done!

Wine Glass Candleholders

Save some wine glasses to help light up your night. These Santa-style candleholders are so simple to make and will dress up your dining room table with holiday delight!

SUPPLIES

Black velvet trim

Candle

Clear mica flakes

Glue gun

Gold buckle

Decoupage glue

Spoon

Spray paint

White pompom trim

Wine glasses

INSTRUCTIONS

1. Spray each wine glass a different color; use two coats of paint for each.

2. Make Santa's belt out of a gold buckle and a black velvet trim, and hot-glue it around the widest part of the glass.

3. Hot-glue white pompom trim around the bottom edge of the glass (which is now the top).

4. Apply decoupage glue to the bottom of the glass, and then use a spoon to sprinkle mica onto the decoupage.

5. Add a candle to the top.

6. Create a matching Santa candle set or find different embellishments for Frosty and gold candle holders.

Glass-Block Gift Lights

Create a few glass-block gifts to light up your party or give away as gifts to your guests. These are simple to make and take under an hour to create!

SUPPLIES

Clear LED light strand: 25–30 bulbs

Decorations

Hot glue gun

Long-shaft screwdriver: at least 8" long

Glass block with pre-drilled hole at bottom: 8" x 8" x 3"

Ribbons

Shredded cellophane: 1 package

Soda straw

White duct tape

Wire-edged ribbon: at least 2 yds long and 2" wide

INSTRUCTIONS

1. Lay the glass block flat on your work surface. Using a screwdriver, start pushing the strand of lights into the block; try to get them to form an "S" in the block. Push about one-third of the lights inside.

2. Push about one-third of the shredded cellophane into the block using the screwdriver. Spread it evenly among the lights to help keep them spaced near the top of the block.

3. Continue to alternate lights and cellophane until you reach the end of the lights in the strand. Pack cellophane at the bottom to help hold everything in place. You will be left with just the cord and plug extending from the hole.

4. Snap the plastic cord keeper into the hole; if the block did not come with one, place white duct tape over the hole.

5. Wrap a long piece of ribbon around the narrow edge of the block and hot-glue it in place.

6. Make a ribbon bow for the top edge of the block and hot-glue it in place.

7. Hot-glue the pick into the center of the bow and attach a decoration to the front of the block. Plug in the lights and behold your creation!

Wine Bottle Cozy

Dress up your wine bottle with some holiday cheer. All you need to make this cute wine bottle cozy is some festive adornments and your favorite bottle of wine. Cheers!

SUPPLIES

Wine bottle

White paper

Pencil

Felt pieces: 2 colors

Sweater

Hat

Pompom trim

Glue gun

Foam snowflake

INSTRUCTIONS

1. Lay a wine bottle down on a piece of white paper. Loosely draw a shirt with sleeves to fit around the neck and body of the bottle. Draw the shirt with an extra 1–1½-inch width on both sides. Cut out the paper shirt and fold it in half. Trim the design to make it symmetrical.

2. Fold a piece of felt in half. Fold the shirt in half again, line it up with the felt fold, and cut out a front piece. Repeat, cutting out a back piece from a different color of felt.

3. Cut up an old hat to create a design for the front of the shirt. Stitch sweater band to the front. Sew the front and back of the shirt together at the sides, leaving the arm holes open. Turn the shirt inside out. Roll up the sides of the sleeves, and hand-sew pompom trim to the front and around the neck.

4. Hot-glue a foam snowflake to the front.

Wine Glass Cozy

Dazzle your favorite wine glass with some ugly bling! This little cozy crochets up quickly so your co-workers won't know how much wine you're sipping at the company party.

SUPPLIES

Worsted weight yarn: 3, 20-yd lengths in different colors

Crochet hook: 5mm (size H-8)

Darning needle

Abbrevation lists: page 124

INSTRUCTIONS

With MC, ch 20 and join in round with sl st.

Round 1: ch1, 20 sc, sl st to join.

Round 2: ch2, *3 dc, 2 dc in next st, rep from * to end, sl st to join (25 sts).

Round 3: ch1, 25 sc, sl st to join with CC1. Cut MC yarn.

Round 4: ch1, 25 sc, sl st to join.

Round 5: ch2, *4 dc, 2 dc in next st, rep from * to end, sl st to join (30 sts).

Round 6: ch1, 30 sc, sl st to join with CC2. Cut CC1 yar.

Round 7: ch1, *5 sc, 2 sc in next st, rep from * to end, sl st to join (35 sts).

Round 8: ch1, 35 hdc, sl st to join.

Round 9: ch1, *6 sc, 2 sc in next st, rep from * to end, sl st to join with CC1 (40 sts). Cut CC2 yarn.

Round 10: ch1, 40 sc, sl st to join.

Round 11: ch2, 40 dc, sl st to join.

Round 12: ch1, 40 sc, sl st to join with MC.

Round 13: ch1, 40 sc, sl st to join.

Round 14: ch2, *8 dc, dc2tog, rep from * to end, sl st to join (36 sts). Cut CC1 yarn.

Round 15: ch1, *7 sc, sc2tog, rep from * to end, sl st to join (32 sts). Cut MC yarn.

Weave in all ends.

Reindeer Beer Bottle Cozies

These Beer Bottle Cozies are so simple to make. They will keep your fingers warm while you hold on to your icy beer during cold winter nights.

SUPPLIES

Worsted weight yarn: 50 yds main color, 20 yds contrasting color and 10 yards accent color(s)

Knitting needles: 4mm (size 6 U.S.) double pointed needles

Stitch marker

Darning needle

Pompoms: ¼"

Abbrevation lists: page 124

INSTRUCTIONS

CO 44 sts. Join in the round, being careful not to twist it. Place marker for beginning of round.

Rounds 1-5: K1, P1 ribbing.

Rounds 6-34, follow color chart beginning on round 1 of chart, repeating chart twice per round.

Bottle Neck

Round 35: *K3, K2tog, rep from * to last 4 sts, K4 (36 sts).

Round 36: K.

Round 37: *K2, K2tog, rep from * to end (27 sts).

Round 38: K.

Round 39: *K1, K2tog, rep from * to end (18 sts).

Round 40: K.

Rounds 41–47: K1, P1 ribbing.

Bind off in pattern, and weave in the ends.

Sew a small red pompom onto the tip of the reindeer's nose to make him glow.

Key

Brown
Red
White

29
28
27
26
25
24
23
22
21
20
19
18
17
16
15
14
13
12
11
10
9
8
7
6
5
4
3
2
1

22 21 20 19 18 17 16 15 14 13 12 11 10 9 8 7 6 5 4 3 2 1

Key

Brown
Green
Navy
White

29
28
27
26
25
24
23
22
21
20
19
18
17
16
15
14
13
12
11
10
9
8
7
6
5
4
3
2
1

22 21 20 19 18 17 16 15 14 13 12 11 10 9 8 7 6 5 4 3 2 1

Festive Tree Beer Bottle Cozies

Decorate your favorite beverage with these festive cozies. Add some bling to make them bright, and pair them with your favorite ugly sweater for some delight!

SUPPLIES

Worsted weight yarn: 50 yds main color, 20 yds contrasting color and 10 yards accent color(s)

Knitting needles: 4mm (size 6 U.S.) double pointed needles

Stitch marker

Darning needle

Pompoms: ¼"

Abbrevation lists: page 124

INSTRUCTIONS

CO 44 sts. Join in the round, being careful not to twist it. Place marker for beginning of round.

Rounds 1-5: K1, P1 ribbing.

Rounds 6-34, follow color chart beginning on round 1 of chart, repeating chart twice per round.

Bottle Neck

Round 35: *K3, K2tog, rep from * to last 4 sts, K4 (36 sts).

Round 36: K.

Round 37: *K2, K2tog, rep from * to end (27 sts).

Round 38: K.

Round 39: *K1, K2tog, rep from * to end (18 sts).

Round 40: K.

Rounds 41–47: K1, P1 ribbing.

Bind off in pattern, and weave in the ends.

Sew random pompoms onto the Christmas tree for decoration.

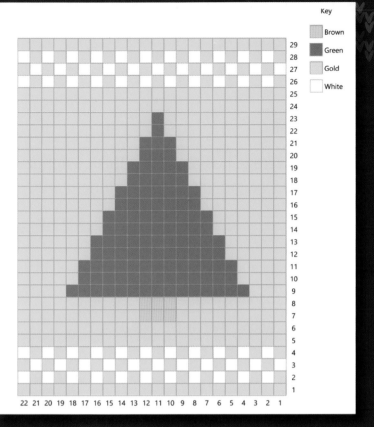

Key

- Brown
- Green
- Gold
- White

29 28 27 26 25 24 23 22 21 20 19 18 17 16 15 14 13 12 11 10 9 8 7 6 5 4 3 2 1

22 21 20 19 18 17 16 15 14 13 12 11 10 9 8 7 6 5 4 3 2 1

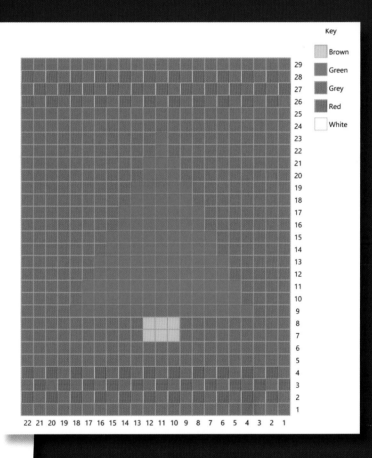

Key

- Brown
- Green
- Grey
- Red
- White

29 28 27 26 25 24 23 22 21 20 19 18 17 16 15 14 13 12 11 10 9 8 7 6 5 4 3 2 1

22 21 20 19 18 17 16 15 14 13 12 11 10 9 8 7 6 5 4 3 2 1

 Beer Can Cozies

The perfect crocheted cozy for your favorite canned beverage has arrived in this customizable, easy-to-make pattern. Just pick out your ugliest worsted weight yarn and combine it with some sparkly yarn to make it your own.

SUPPLIES

Worsted weight yarn: various colors, approximately 25 yards of each color

Crochet hook: 5mm (size H-8)

Darning needle

Abbreviation lists: page 124

INSTRUCTIONS

All Cozies (Base)

With MC ch 3, sl st to join.

Base Round 1: ch1 in center of ring, 8 sc, sl st to join (8 sts).

Round 2: ch1, 2 sc in each sc of previous round, sl st to join (16 sts).

Round 3: ch1, *1 sc in next st, 2 sc in next st, rep from * around, sl st to join (24 sts).

Round 4: ch1, *2 sc in each of next 2 sts, 2 sc in next st, rep from * around, sl st to join (32 sts).

Work only in back loops from this point forward.

Round 5: sc in each st around, sl st to join.

Round 6: hdc in each st around, sl st to join with CC1.

Tri-Colored Cozy (gold, green, and red)

Round 7: ch2, dc in each st, sl st to join with CC2. Cut CC1 yarn.

Round 8: ch2, dc in each st, sl st to join with CC1. Cut CC2 yarn.

Round 9: ch2, dc in each st, sl st to join with MC. Cut CC1 yarn.

Round 10: ch2, dc in each st, sl st to join with CC1. Cut MC yarn.

Repeat rounds 7–9 one more time.

Weave in all ends.

Christmas Stripes Cozy (green, red, and white)

Round 7: ch2, dc in each st, sl st to join with CC2. Cut CC1 yarn.

Round 8: ch1, sc in each st, sl st to join with CC1. Cut CC2 yarn.

Repeat rounds 7–8 four more times. Repeat round 7

Weave in all ends.

Jingle Bell Stripes Cozy (blue, green, white, and red)

Round 7: ch2, dc in each st, sl st to join with CC2. Cut CC1 yarn.

Round 8: ch1, sc in each st, sl st to join with CC3. Cut CC2 yarn.

Round 9: ch2, dc in each st, sl st to join.

Round 10: ch2, dc in each st, sl st to join with CC2. Cut CC3 yarn.

Rounds 11–13 repeat rounds 8–10 one more time

Round 14: ch1, sc in each st, sl st to join with CC1. Cut CC2 yarn.

Round 15: ch2, dc in each st, sl st to join with MC. Cut CC1 yarn.

Round 16: ch1, hdc in each st, sl st to join. Cut MC yarn.

Weave in all ends.

White Christmas Stripes Cozy (white, brown, and red)

Round 7: ch2, dc in each st, sl st to join.

Round 8: ch2, dc in each st, sl st to join with MC. Cut CC1 yarn.

Round 9: ch2, dc in each st, sl st to join with CC2. Cut MC yarn.

Round 10: ch2, dc in each st, sl st to join.

Round 11: ch2, dc in each st, sl st to join with MC. Cut CC2 yarn.

Round 12: ch2, dc in each st, sl st to join with CC1. Cut MC yarn.

Rounds 13 and 14: ch2, dc in each st, sl st to join. Cut CC1 yarn.

Weave in all ends.

 Rein-Beers

These cute little reindeer beers are easy as can be! So fun and festive, they are sure to punch up any table design. You can also give them as parting gifts to your ugly-sweater-wearing guests.

SUPPLIES

Beer bottle

Brown pipe cleaner

Hot glue

Googly eyes

Small red pompom

INSTRUCTIONS

1. Wrap a pipe cleaner around the top of a beer bottle; twist and turn the ends up at the back.

2. Cut the excess pipe cleaner that is sticking up to the desired antler length.

3. Wrap the cut-off pipe cleaner pieces onto the wrapped pipe cleaners to make the smaller antler sections.

4. Hot-glue the googly eyes and red pompom nose onto the bottle. (Note: You can find the beer bottle labels on page 114.)

66

Plate Photo Backdrop

Tape these plate strands to your ceiling to create a foolproof backdrop for funny photos and polaroids. You can prompt your guests to bring props—like mustaches, beards, hats, and glasses—to make the pictures even more priceless, or learn how to make your own on page 66.

SUPPLIES

Craft knife or mini hole punch

Glue gun

Paper plates: red and green

White yarn

INSTRUCTIONS

1. Stack a red and a green paper plate on top of each other, and punch through the top and bottom of both.

2. Thread white yarn through the holes, and continue to add additional hole-punched plates to the strand, spacing them out, until it reaches your desired length.

3. Place a small dab of hot glue around the hole on the backside of each plate to keep it from rotating.

Ugly Photo Props

What's an ugly sweater party without hilarious photos to remember the night? In case your memory fails you due to the delicious drinks you've brewed, make sure to take plenty of pictures with fun props. These are so simple to make, and your guests will thank you providing them to the party!

SUPPLIES

Arrow graphics

Matte printer paper: 13" x 19"

Craft knife

Foam core poster board

Glue gun

Ink-jet printer

Scissors

Spray adhesive

Sweater scraps

Ugly Christmas sweater clip art

Wooden sticks

INSTRUCTIONS

1. To create a bow tie, trim a small strip of a sweater scrap and adhere the ends together. Trim a smaller alternate color of sweater. Fold it in half, and wrap it around the center of the previous piece Adhere a wooden stick to the back of the bow tie.

2. Print graphics onto 13" x 19" paper and cut out. Spray the backs of printouts with spray adhesive, and mount them onto foam core poster board. Trim around the graphics with a craft knife. Hot-glue a wooden stick to the back of each piece. *(Note: You can find the ugly invitation on page 121.)*

IT'S GONNA GET UGLY!
YOU'RE INVITED TO BREAK OUT YOUR VERY WORST
AT THE JONESES' ANNUAL

UGLY SWEATER PARTY
FRIDAY, DECEMBER 12TH AT 7:00PM

THE JONES RESIDENCE

UGLY

UGLIER

HO HO

Sweater Voting Box

This project looks much harder than it actually is, but you're essentially slipping and fitting a sweater over a box. This adornment will liven up your holiday décor even more while providing a perfect place for your guests to vote for the ugliest sweater.

SUPPLIES

Bell necklace

Box

Box cutter

Glue gun

Green glitter cardstock

Paper trimmer

Pens

Printer

Red turtleneck sweater

Scissors

INSTRUCTIONS

1. Place a box inside of a sweater, and center it underneath the turtleneck.

2. Hot-glue the sweater to the box, just around the neckline. Cut up both sides of the sweater to the armpits. Wrap the sweater around the box, trim off the excess fabric, and then hot-glue in place.

3. With the box cutter, cut an opening in the box inside of the turtleneck.

4. Print out the words "Vote Here" with some holiday graphics, trim to size, and hot-glue onto green cardstock.

5. Cut the panel into a circle and hot-glue in onto the front of the sweater. Drape a bell necklace around the neck of the sweater. Place the voting box on a surface.

6. Trim voting ballets and place them in a folded sleeve of the sweater. Fold the opposite sleeve of the sweater to create a cup to hold pens. *(Note: Remember this is an "ugly sweater" box, so don't be too concerned about imperfections.)*

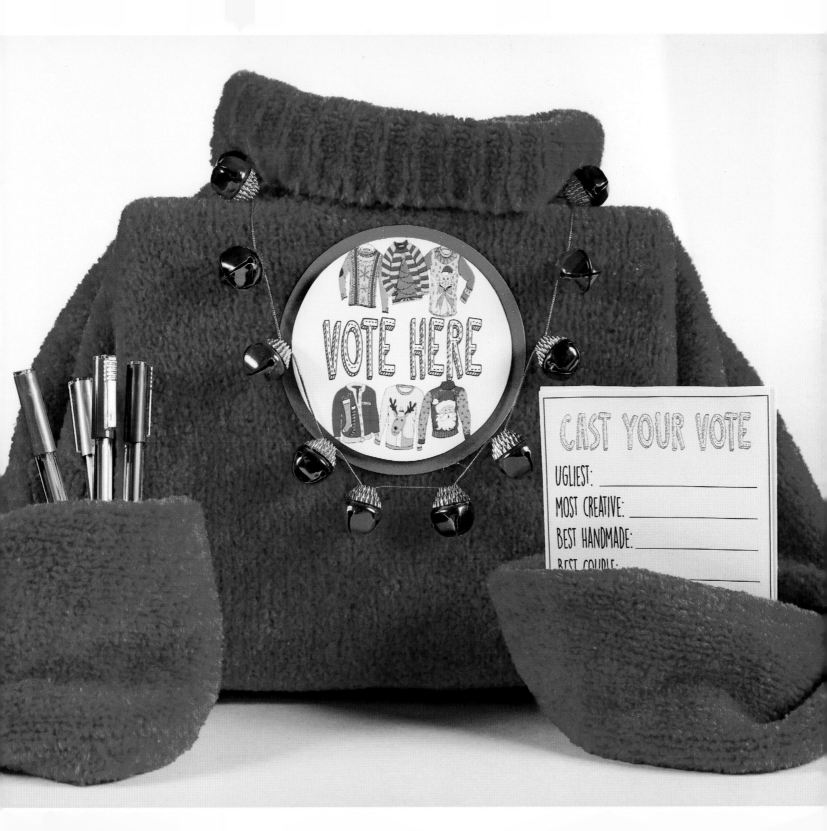

Naughty or Nice

Ugly Apparel

Jingle Bells Sweater

This playful sweater is the perfect amount of noisy and nice. Its silly sentiment will put pressure on your guests to up their ugly sweater game.

SUPPLIES

Assorted bells

Black men's sweater

Glue gun

Needle and thread

Tinsel pipe cleaners: silver, gold, and metallic-green

INSTRUCTIONS

1. Bend pipe cleaners to spell out "Jingle Bells," and hot-glue them onto the sweater.

2. Sew each bell to the front of the sweater and sleeves as desired; alternate colors and sizes to add variety. *(Note: You can also hot-glue the bells onto the sweater, but be careful not to glue the inside so they will keep jingling.)*

Snow Globe Sweater

Using a plastic bowl, candies, some feathers, and pompoms, you can trap Frosty in a snow globe on the front of your sweater!

SUPPLIES

Clear plastic bowl

Glue gun

Green feather boa

Needle and thread

Peppermint candies

Pompons: white and silver

Red sweater

Stuffed snowman ornament

Decorative snow: small and large

INSTRUCTIONS

1. Hot-glue the stuffed snowman ornament to the center of the sweater.

2. Carefully place decorative snow and pompoms around the snowman.

3. Hot-glue a clear bowl onto the sweater around the snowman, pompoms, and snow.

4. Hide the edge of bowl by hot-gluing the boa around it.

5. Adhere additional peppermint candies onto the sweater.

#

Use this design to call even more attention to your holiday sweater. Keep the sweater and adornments in a gray-and-red color scheme to really make the green wreaths stand out!

SUPPLIES

Glue gun

Gray sweater

Mini glitter wreaths: 2

Needle and thread

Red beaded garland

Red jingle jells

Red mini ornaments

Red tinsel garland

INSTRUCTIONS

1. Cut mini glitter wreaths and bend open to hot-glue around bottom of sweater.

2. Hot-glue a red tinsel garland around the neck of the sweater and around the cuffs.

3. Cut beads off of the beaded garland, and position them around the front of the sweater.

4. Place red jingle bells and mini ornaments onto the front of sweater.

5. Once happy with the placement of the small beads, bells, and ornaments, hot-glue them all in place. *(Note: You can sew the mini ornaments in place instead of gluing them if you'd like them to sway.)*

Light-Up Christmas Tree Sweater

Here's your second chance to ugly up a tree this year. Consider using flashing lights, dangling mini ornaments, popcorn, and more!

SUPPLIES

Assorted mini ornaments

Glue gun

Gray sweater

Green tinsel garland

Mini battery-operated light strands

Scissors

Tinsel

INSTRUCTIONS

1. Lay the tinsel garland on the sweater to determine placement, and then hot-glue it in place.

2. Poke lights from the inside through the outside of the sweater. Hot-glue the lights in place, and hot-glue the battery pack to the inside bottom edge of the sweater.

3. Add mini ornaments to the garland by simply removing the wire hook from the tops, and then threading them over the garland and back inside of the ornaments. This will allow the ornaments to move freely with the sweater.

4. Carefully thread tinsel over and under the garland.

5. Hot-glue a tree topper on top of the tree.

Decorated Christmas Tree Sweater

This adorably adorned sweater provides both entertainment and treats. Get creative with the adornments and candy, consider wearing it with a Star Headband (page 94), and make sure to have your friends each eat a candy cane hanging from the tree!

SUPPLIES

Assorted plastic ornaments

Candy canes

Glue gun

Green sweatshirt or sweater

Tinsel garlands: green
and multicolored

Twine or yarn

INSTRUCTIONS

1. Hot-glue the tinsel along the front of the sweater and along the arms.

2. Tie ornaments to the garland using twine or yarn.

3. Hang candy canes, multicolored tinsel, and an assortment of ugly ornaments onto the garland tree.

Oh "Deer," That's an Ugly Sweater!

You will be the talk of the town in this frightful sweater! The deer head sweater will always be a classic and is easy to do!

SUPPLIES

Cardboard: 2, 10" x 10" pieces

Pencil

Stuffed animal deer

Ugly sweater

INSTRUCTIONS

1. Use scissors to cut a deer stuffed animal in half. Trace the outer edge of the deer head onto a piece of cardboard using a pencil and cut out.

2. Cut the cardboard to match the diameter size of deer head.

3. Pull and tuck the edges of the cut deer head over and around the piece of cardboard.

4. Hot-glue the cardboard deer head onto the front of the sweater.

5. Repeat the above steps with the back half of the deer stuffed animal and the back of the sweater.

X-MAS PONCHO

You'll be comfortable and cozy as can be in this X-mas Poncho. The more flowers you add, the better!

SUPPLIES

Assorted silk flowers

Christmas tree skirt

Felt

Glue gun

Pompom trim: about 5 yds

Resin flower centers

Ribbon

Small paper flowers

INSTRUCTIONS

1. Sew pompom trim around the bottom and neck hole of the tree skirt.

2. Cut leaf shapes from felt, and hot-glue them onto the tree skirt.

3. Remove the plastic parts of the silk flowers so you are left with the petals. Layer assorted petals together, pin them onto the skirt, and then hot-glue them in place.

4. Add small paper flowers and resin flower centers for the centers of the flowers. *(Note: You can find items like these at any craft store.)*

5. To finish, simply sew two lengths of ribbon to each side of the back of the neck, and tie it on!

POINSETTIA PONCHO

This poinsettia poncho is incredibly simple to make and only calls for three supplies. Throw poinsettias onto the sweater, and then throw it over your head.

SUPPLIES

Assorted poinsettias

Glue gun

Green poncho

INSTRUCTIONS

1. Place various sizes and styles of poinsettias diagonally across the front of the poncho.

2. Once you are happy with the placement of the poinsettias, hot-glue them in place.

89

Christmas Tree Skirt!

When it's finally time to buy a new tree skirt, don't throw away your old one . . . repurpose it into a hideous skirt of your own so you and your Christmas tree can match! With all the flowers, stars, and buttons, you should wear this skirt with pride instead of hiding it underneath all the presents!

SUPPLIES

Assorted buttons

Embroidery needle

Fabric die-cut machine and flower die-cut

Felt: 72", ⅓ yd white and ⅓ yd red

Glitter iron-on vinyl

Gold lame fabric: ⅛ yd

Large button

Large white rickrack: 2½ yds

Needle and thread

Pre-cut felt pieces: 3 white snowflakes and 5 red stars

Red embroidery floss: 1 skein

Red felt tree skirt

Sewing machine

Silhouette craft cutter

INSTRUCTIONS

1. Measure your waist; draw a circle with that circumference onto paper and cut out. Use this as a template to cut a circle out of the center of the skirt.

2. Sew the pompom trim around the skirt, and sew rickrack around the waist and down the two back seams.

3. Using a craft cutter, cut "Merry & Bright" out of gold glitter vinyl. Iron the text onto the skirt following the manufacturer's instructions.

4. Die-cut six red flowers from red felt. Cut sixteen large circles and three small circles from gold fabric, and cut five smaller from red felt.

5. Layer and hand-sew all of the circles, flowers, and buttons onto the skirt.

6. Stitch the snowflakes onto the skirt.

7. Sew a large button onto the back of the skirt at the waist. Create a button-loop closure on the opposite side of the button.

Christmas Tree Dress

SUPPLIES

Glue gun

Lime-green crocheted headband
trim: 9" wide, 1½ yds

Lime-green tulle: 54" wide, 20 yds

Mini ornaments: 2 assorted tubes

Needle and thread

Plastic candy canes

Poinsettias

Red sparkly tulle: 54" wide, ½ yd

Sewing machine

Sparkly ornaments: medium size,
6 red and 6 gold

INSTRUCTIONS

1. Measure the lime-green crocheted headband trim to fit your bust size, mark the length with a pin, and then cut and machine-sew the ends together to form a tube top. Fit the tube top over the back of a kitchen chair; this will make it easier to add the tulle.

2. Starting at the fold of the fabric, cut 6-inch strips of lime-green tulle; they will be 54 inches long if you cut from the fold. *(Note: You will use all 20 yards, so it's better to cut it all at once.)*

3. To form the skirt, slipknot tulle strips to the bottom of the crocheted headband trim at every other hole until you have circled the skirt. *(Note: There are many videos online that demonstrate this technique.)*

4. Repeat this slipknot technique at the top of the dress, but instead of letting the ends fall, pull them though the remaining holes on the skirt.

6. Hot-glue the ornaments and poinsettias to the top as shown. Be very careful with this step; Use finger protectors (available at many craft and DIY stores) to avoid burning yourself. Glue three poinsettias onto the belt.

7. Tie mini ornaments in random places around the skirt using the thin gold thread that comes with the ornaments.

8. Tie candy canes to the skirt using the tulle.

5. For the straps and belt, cut three 6-inch pieces of red tulle in the same manner as you cut the green tulle–on the fold. Try the dress on to determine a comfortable placement, and then trim them to size. Attach the straps to the dress by adding a slipknot, knotting them in place on the front, and then tying them in the back. Don't worry if any tulle is showing; the ornaments and poinsettias will later cover it. For the belt, simply tie the last long red tulle strip around the waist.

STAR HEADBAND

Just like a tacky tree topper will complete your Christmas tree, this star headband will tie together your ugly ensemble.

SUPPLIES

Glue gun

Gold tinsel garland

Gold tree star

Headband

Heavy-duty craft wire

INSTRUCTIONS

1. Using the craft wire, wire-wrap the gold tree star to the top of the headband and make sure it is secure.

2. Cut a length of garland to cover the headband, and glue it down using the glue gun. If you can still see wire, add another piece of garland with the glue gun to cover it.

CHRISTMAS ORNAMENT HEADBAND

Top off your look with a festive holiday headband. And when we say festive, we mean it! With ornaments atop your head, you'll be the talk of the party!

SUPPLIES

Glue gun

Gold tinsel garland

Headband

Plastic Christmas ornaments

INSTRUCTIONS

1. Carefully hot-glue Christmas ornaments to a headband.

2. Cut a length of garland, wrap it around the ornaments and the headband, and hot-glue it in place.

GLITTER POINSETTIA SHOES

Put your best foot forward in these glittered high heels. You'll feel festive as can be while flaunting these on your feet!

SUPPLIES

Foam brush

Green chunky glitter

Hairspray

High-heeled shoes

Decoupage glue

Poinsettia ornament clips

INSTRUCTIONS

1. Coat small sections of shoes with decoupage glue and sprinkle glitter on top. Continue until the entire shoes are glittered. Let dry.

2. Add another coat of decoupage and glitter, and let dry completely overnight.

3. Seal the shoes with hairspray to keep the glitter intact.

4. Add poinsettia clips to the fronts of the shoes.

Red Christmas Shoes

Treat your feet as a Christmas tree this year, and dress them with ornaments, glitter, tinsel, and cheer.

SUPPLIES

Foam ornaments

Glue gun

Mini glitter

Mini tinsel garland

Red shoes

INSTRUCTIONS

1. Hot-glue a mini tinsel garland along the opening of the shoes.

2. Sporadically hot-glue mini foam ornaments along edges of shoes. If needed, cut foam balls in half to create clusters.

#

Accessories can make the outfit. Ornament yourself from head to toe with these comfy and easy-to-make leg warmers.

SUPPLIES

Flower buttons

Old sweater

Trims: 1 polka-dot and 1 ruffled

Sewing machine

INSTRUCTIONS

1. Depending on the width and stretch of the sweater sleeves, you can either cut off the sleeves to use as the leg warmer base, or use the front or back panel of the sweater. If using the front or back of the sweater, cut two 12-inch-wide panels that are 12–18 inches long, depending on the length you need. Fold each piece in half length-wise with right sides facing.

2. Pin two coordinating trims in between the front and back of the leg warmer.

3. Fold the polka-dot trim in half length-wise and then pin it in place. Turn the leg warmer inside out.

4. Remove the plastic centers from the silk flowers so you are left with the petals. Stitch an assortment of flowers with a button center onto the top of each leg warmer.

Ugly Pooch

Don't forget to dress up your dog in an ugly sweater this holiday season. Take a trip to your local thrift store for a cheap find that will make your pup look extra fancy once uglied-up.

SUPPLIES

Glue gun

Green felt

Old sweater

Pompom balls: assorted sizes and colors

Pompom trim

INSTRUCTIONS

1. Try the sweater on your dog to see how it fits.

2. Take in the sides or neck of the sweater as needed.

3. Cut a Christmas tree out of green felt, pin it to the backside of the sweater, and stitch it in place.

4. Pin pompom trim across the tree and stitch in place. Hot-glue pompom balls onto the tree.

GETTIN' UGLY GAMES

Marshmallow Pickup

Soft and fluffy and everything puffy–this game is sure to be a hit! Steady hands are key to this game, or else you may run into some trouble.

SUPPLIES

Bags of mini marshmallows

Chopsticks: 1 set for each team

Cups or containers: 1 for each player

INSTRUCTIONS

1. Divide everyone up into teams of two. Each team stands opposite of the team they will compete against at a table.

2. Place a pile of marshmallows on the table in the middle of each competing team, and give each player a set of chopsticks and a cup or container.

3. Set the timer for 1 minute. Player one from each team picks up as many mini marshmallows with chopsticks as he or she can.

4. Reset the timer, and player two from each team takes a turn.

5. The teams with the most marshmallows win.

STRUT THE UGLY CAT WALK

Here's your last chance to get everyone's attention; strut it ugly and proud to show you deserve to win the honor of ugliest outfit.

INSTRUCTIONS

1. Divide your guests in half and have them stand on either side of the room.

2. Crank some fun and funky music.

3. Each person takes a turn strutting their stuff down the center.

4. After the fashion show, everyone casts a vote for ugliest ensemble in an ugly sweater ballot box.

5. Give out awards for ugliest outfits! *(Note: You can find the ballot box on page 69 and the badges on page 122.)*

Hideous White Elephant Gift Exchange

Hold on tight to your ugly sweater for this knee-slapping good time. All the prep you need is to request that each guest bring a wrapped naughty (gag) or nice gift with no nametag; that way, the giver of each pleasant or unpleasant gift is kept a secret.

SUPPLIES

Gifts

Hat or bowl

Pens and paper

INSTRUCTIONS

1. As the host or hostess, make sure to count the number of guests who brought a gift. Cut that many squares of paper and number them.

2. Fold and put squares in a hat or bowl. Each guest picks a number. Whoever drew number one chooses a gift and opens it in front of the party.

3. The person who drew number two can then either steal the already opened gift or open a wrapped gift. Then it is number three's turn, and so on.

4. Once a person's gift is stolen, he or she can either steal someone else's gift or open a new one.

Blindfolded Ugly Wrap

Those late nights spent sneakily wrapping presents from Santa will come in handy for this game. The team with the best wrap-job on their present wins; but, just so you know . . . you will be blindfolded.

SUPPLIES

Bows	Scissors
Odd-shaped gifts: 1 for each team	Tags
Pens	Tape
Ribbon	Wrapping paper

INSTRUCTIONS

1. Request for four volunteers to be judges. Divide the remaining contestants into teams of two.

2. Blindfold each contestant. Place an odd-shaped gift and all the wrapping fixings in front of each team.

3. Set a timer for 3 minutes, during which each team must work together to wrap their gift.

4. The judges select the winning team based on accuracy and creativity.

Ugly Ornament Gift Exchange

This game tends to bring out the naughty, not nice, in all of the guests. The good news: Everyone will bring home an ugly ornament for their tree, even if it costs them their dignity! Just have each guest bring one wrapped ugly ornament to the party.

SUPPLIES

Bowl

Pens and paper

Wrapped ornaments

INSTRUCTIONS

1. Each guest writes a secret or confession on a piece of paper and folds it up.

2. Put each secret in a bowl and each ugly ornament under the tree.

3. The first player pulls a secret out of the bowl, reads it aloud, and has one chance to guess who wrote it. If the player guesses correctly, he or she grabs an ugly ornament; if incorrect, it is the next player's turn to guess that secret. This continues until someone guesses the secret correctly, who then can grab an ugly ornament.

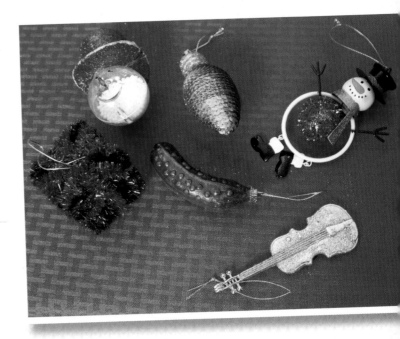

4. The next player then picks and reads a secret aloud. This continues until all the ornaments are gone.

5. The person with the most ugly ornaments at the end of the game is the winner.

Candy Cane Pickup

Visions of candy canes will be dancing in your head after this funny game! Grab your teammate and get your game faces on . . . it is time to pull in a win!

SUPPLIES

Candy canes

Cups or containers: 1 for each team

INSTRUCTIONS

1. Place a pile of candy canes in the middle of the table for each couple going head-to-head, and give each player a candy cane and a cup or container.

2. Set the timer for 1 minute, during which player one from each team hooks as many candy canes from the pile as possible with only the hook part of his or her candy cane.

3. Start the timer again for player two from each team to take a turn.

4. The team with the most candy canes wins.

Kiss the Ugly Stocking

Nimble fingers won't help you with this competition; you will have ugly Christmas stockings on your hands to make sure of that! Keep your eye on the prize and you just might come out on top.

SUPPLIES

Candies wrapped in foil   Ugly Christmas stockings: 2 for each team

INSTRUCTIONS

1. Divide everyone into teams of two.

2. Player one from each team puts stockings on their hands while player two stands across a table.

3. Place a pile of wrapped candies in front of player one. Set a timer for 1 minute, during which player one unwraps the candy one by one and tries to toss them into player two's mouth.

4. The team that catches the most candies wins.

CONGRATULATIONS, YOU'RE THE UGLIEST WINNER

UGLY Bubbly

UGLY ALE Beer TASTES FOR AGES

BIRRA · BEER · ALUS · OLUT · CERVEZA · BIRA · BAKUSHU · PIWO · BIRRE · BIER · OL · BIER · CERVEJA

RED NOSE ALE

Beer Bottle Labels

Give your favorite brew an ugly sweater twist with these hideous little wraps. Labels available for download at *larkcrafts.com/bonus*.

Wine Bottle Labels

Let your vino-loving friends know that you pick only the best from the ugliest of regions. Labels available for download at *larkcrafts.com/bonus*.

HIDEOUS CHÂTEAUX
Winey Little White
2015

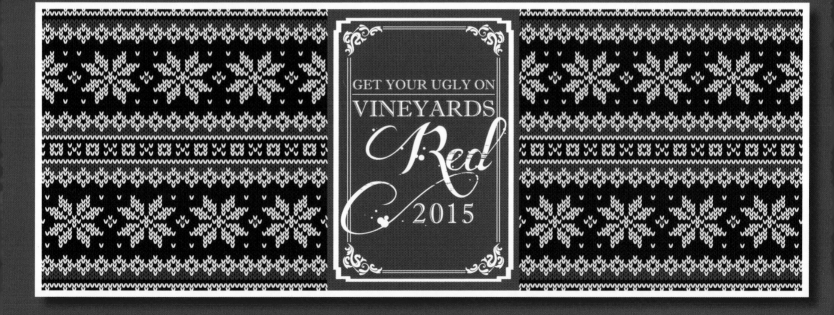

GET YOUR UGLY ON
VINEYARDS
Red
2015

CHAMPAGNE BOTTLE LABELS

Pop the cork on this "Ugly Bubbly" and let the party get started! Labels available for download at *larkcrafts.com/bonus*.

UGLY
Bubbly

UGLY-VITATIONS

You have to let your guests know it's about to get ugly, and what better way than with an ugly invitation? Invites available for download at *larkcrafts.com/bonus*.

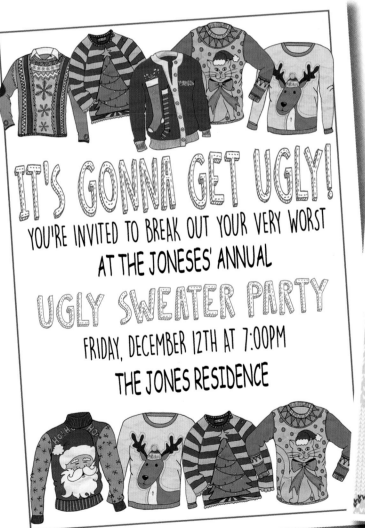

IT'S GONNA GET UGLY!
YOU'RE INVITED TO BREAK OUT YOUR VERY WORST AT THE JONESES' ANNUAL
UGLY SWEATER PARTY
FRIDAY, DECEMBER 12TH AT 7:00PM
THE JONES RESIDENCE

YOU'RE INVITED TO OUR
UGLY SWEATER PARTY
EAT, DRINK & BE UGLY

HOST: Cassie & Nick
PLACE: 1729 N. 925 E.
DATE & TIME: Dec. 15th, 7:00pm

AWARDS

Let your guests know they're the ugliest with these ugly badges. Just glue some ribbon and a pin to the back, and you're good to get ugly. Awards available for download at *larkcrafts.com/bonus*.

CONGRATULATIONS, YOU'RE
UGLIER
MOST CREATIVE

CONGRATULATIONS, YOU'RE THE
UGLIEST
WINNER

KNITTING ABBREVATIONS

CO: cast on

K: knit

K2tog: knit 2 together

P: purl

rep: repeat

st(s): stitch(es)

CROCHET ABBREVATIONS

CC1: contrast color 1

CC2: contrast color 2

ch: chain stitch

dc: double crochet

dc2tog: double crochet 2 sts together

hdc: half double crochet

MC: main color

rep: repeat

sc: single crochet

sc2tog: single crochet 2 sts together

sl st: slip stitch

st: stitch

TEMPERATURE CONVERSION

Fahrenheit	Celsius
32°	0°
212°	100°
250°	121°
275°	135°
300°	149°
350°	177°
375°	191°
400°	204°
425°	218°

METRIC CONVERSION CHART BY VOLUME (FOR LIQUIDS)

U.S.	Metric (millimeters/liters)
¼ teaspoon	1.25 mL
½ teaspoon	2.5 mL
1 teaspoon	5 mL
1 tablespoon	15 mL
¼ cup	60 mL
½ cup	120 mL
¾ cup	180 mL
1 cup	240 mL
2 cups (1 pint)	480 mL
4 cups (1 quart)	960 mL
4 quarts (1 gallon)	3.8 L

METRIC CONVERSION CHART BY WEIGHT (FOR DRY INGREDIENTS)

U.S.	Metric (grams/kilograms)
¼ teaspoon	1 g
½ teaspoon	2 g
1 teaspoon	5 g
1 tablespoon	15 g
16 ounces (1 pound)	450 g
2 pounds	900 g
3 pounds	1.4 kg
4 pounds	1.8 kg
5 pounds	2.3 kg
6 pounds	2.7 kg

INDEX

INDEX

Art Director
Matt Shay

Director
Brandy Shay

Photographer
Toni Albrecht
www.tonijstudios.com

Editor
Cynthia Levens

Assistant Editor
Michelle Hainer

Baker
Chelsi Johnston

Knitter
Maggie Fangmann

Crafters:
Lori Allred
Paige Hill
Leanne Shay
Jayme Shepherd

Sweater Illustrations
Carrie Stephens
www.fishscraps.etsy.com

Book Packaged by
Shay Design
www.shaydesign.com